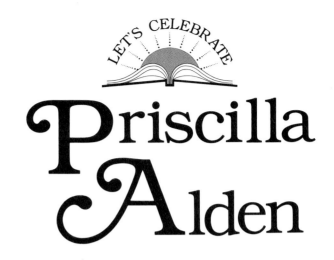

Priscilla Alden

and the First Thanksgiving

by Alice Benjamin Boynton
pictures by Christa Kieffer

Silver Press

Produced by Kirchoff/Wohlberg, Inc.
Text copyright © 1990 Kirchoff/Wohlberg, Inc.
Illustrations copyright © 1990 Christa Kieffer and
Kirchoff/Wohlberg, Inc.

Published by Silver Press, a division of Silver Burdett Press, Inc.
Simon & Schuster, Inc., Prentice Hall Bldg., Englewood Cliffs, NJ 07632

Printed in the United States of America

10 9 8 7 6 5 4 3 2 1

Library of Congress Cataloging-in-Publication Data
Boynton, Alice Benjamin.
Priscilla Alden and the story of the first Thanksgiving / by Alice
Benjamin Boynton; pictures by Christa Kieffer.
p. cm.—(Let's celebrate)
Summary: Describes how Priscilla Alden came to the New World with
the other Pilgrims, helped settle the colony of New Plymouth, and
celebrated the first Thanksgiving.
1. Alden, Priscilla—Juvenile literature. 2. Pilgrims (New
Plymouth Colony)—Biography—Juvenile literature. 3. Massachusetts—
History—New Plymouth, 1620-1691—Juvenile literature.
4. Thanksgiving Day—Juvenile literature. [1. Alden, Priscilla.
2. Pilgrims (New Plymouth Colony) 3. Massachusetts—History—New
Plymouth, 1620-1691 4. Thanksgiving Day.] I. Kieffer, Christa,
ill. II. Title. III. Series.
F68.A346B68 1990   89-49539
394.2'683—dc20   CIP
[92]   AC
ISBN 0-671-69111-2   ISBN 0-671-69105-8 (lib. bdg.)

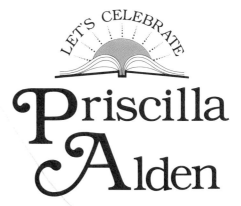

LET'S CELEBRATE

Priscilla Alden

and the First Thanksgiving

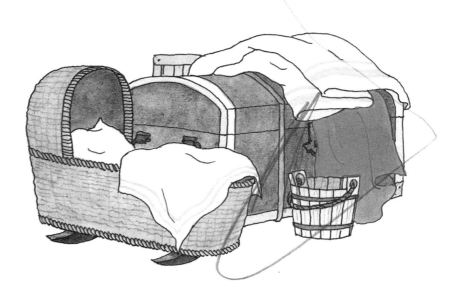

Leaving England

Priscilla sat up in bed.

"I can't sleep!" she said to herself.

For days she had been helping her mother pack. Which things would they take to their new home? Which things would they leave here in England?

Finally the tightly packed trunks and wooden boxes were ready. Why, there was even a crate filled with shoes and boots from her father's shoe shop. He would use them to start a new business in the new land.

"Imagine!" thought Priscilla. "Soon we'll be sailing across the great Atlantic Ocean on the *Mayflower!*"

The *Mayflower* stood ready. On board there were 102 men, women, and children, 30 crewmen, 2 dogs, and the ship's cat.

The passengers took a long, last look at England. Some gathered together to pray to God for a safe trip.

Priscilla's father had said, ''We are going to a new world for a better life. But many of the other families are leaving because the laws in England do not allow them to pray as they wish.''

A sailor shouted, ''Lift anchor! We're away!''

The wind filled the sails. The small ship moved out to sea.

The adventure was beginning!

7

8

Sailing on the *Mayflower*

"Follow me, Priscilla," said Joseph.
He pulled his sister after him.
Joseph bowed to Captain Jones.
He ducked under the boom.
He waved to the sailors.
He hurried by the muskets.
He squeezed past the water barrels.
He poked the dried peas and beans.
"Now you follow me," said Priscilla as
she led him to their parents on the crowded
deck. And so ended their first day at sea.

9

Crash! Lightning flashed across the dark sky.

Boom! The thunder roared.

Icy water dripped everywhere. Priscilla pulled a thin blanket over her wet head. As the ship rolled, she rolled, first to one side, then to the other.

"Ouch!" cried Joseph as she bumped into him.

The boy looked at his sister. "I thought sailing across the ocean would be such fun. But it's not!"

"I know," Priscilla answered. "I feel awful, and I'm always hungry."

Joseph's eyes opened wide. "Are we lost, Priscilla? Do you think we'll all be drowned?"

"Captain Jones will get us to the new land safely," his sister said. But she looked worried, too.

Their mother reached over and patted them. "Be brave," she said. "We've been at sea forty-eight days. We're sure to see land soon. If the weather is fair tomorrow, you can go up on deck."

"You, there! Where are you going?" barked a sailor. Priscilla, Joseph, and young John Howland stopped.

"We want to go up on deck," said John.

"Miles Standish said I could watch him drill the men," said Joseph. "Someday he'll teach me how to march and fire a musket, too."

"There's no drill today!" said the sailor. "It's too dangerous on deck. The waves are high. Stay below!"

"I'm going up anyway," John whispered. "I feel like a goat in a pen!"

Priscilla watched him quietly open a hatch. As he stepped out on deck, he laughed happily. So what if the waves were as high as a house? At last he could breathe fresh, sweet-smelling air.

13

Suddenly the wind made the boat tip way over. A huge wave crashed down on the deck. It washed John into the sea!

"Man overboard!" sailors shouted. They stumbled to the side of the ship.

"He's gone under!"

"No, there he is!"

"Quick, get the boat hook!"

Somehow John had grabbed a rope hanging over the side of the ship. He held on tight. The sailors lowered the hook. Could they reach him?

Still watching, Priscilla held her breath. She saw the sailors pull John out of the water. He could hardly stand up, but he was safe.

The days went by—52, 53, 54. Priscilla tried to keep Joseph busy. "Let's see John Alden," she said one day.

They found John Alden on the lowest deck of the *Mayflower*. He had an important job on ship. Every day, he had to check the water barrels for leaks.

"Have you heard the news?" Priscilla asked John.

"What? Are more people sick?" said John.

"No, this time it's good news. Elizabeth and Stephen Hopkins have a new baby—a boy!"

"That's a blessing," said John. "What's his name?"

"They'll call him Oceanus," said Priscilla, "because he was born on the Atlantic Ocean."

It seemed that the trip would never be over.

When they had been at sea 65 days, a sailor suddenly gave a shout. "LAND! Land Ho!"

It was the call everyone had been waiting to hear. "La-a-a-nd Ho-o-o-o!"

The Pilgrims kneeled and gave thanks to God.

It was November 19, 1620. The brave *Mayflower* passengers had come to the New World at last.

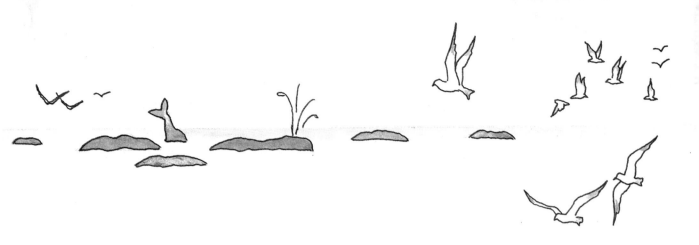

Living in a New Land

The men, women, and children who were not sick went ashore. There was much chatter and laughter. They were happy to be alive.

"I don't even mind doing the wash," said Priscilla.

The children ran on the beach and dug in the sand.

"We've found clams and mussels!" shouted Joseph.

"They'll taste so good after all the salt meat and dried peas we've eaten!" said their mother.

Some of the men, led by Miles Standish, set out to explore the land. "We must see if this is a good place to settle," William Bradford told the Pilgrims.

The men explored for almost three days. They returned to the *Mayflower* tired and cold and wet. Everyone crowded around them.

"We must look for a better place to settle. There is not enough fresh water here," said William Bradford.

The faces around him looked very worried.

Day after day the brave men went out to explore. Time was running out. Winter was at hand.

The Pilgrims lived aboard the *Mayflower.* Many of them were sick. Food and supplies were low.

One day late in December, the explorers returned to the ship, full of excitement.

"We've found a most hopeful place," said Bradford.

"It has many brooks with fresh water," said Alden.

"And there is good black soil for planting and plenty of trees for wood," John Howland said.

"We'll call it Plymouth," said Miles Standish. "We left Plymouth in England. Now we'll live in Plymouth in a new England."

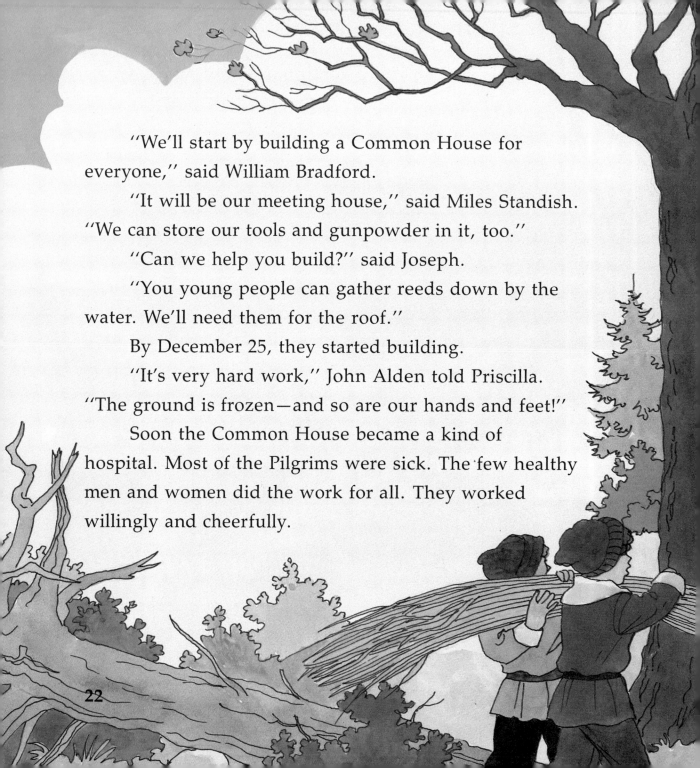

"We'll start by building a Common House for everyone," said William Bradford.

"It will be our meeting house," said Miles Standish. "We can store our tools and gunpowder in it, too."

"Can we help you build?" said Joseph.

"You young people can gather reeds down by the water. We'll need them for the roof."

By December 25, they started building.

"It's very hard work," John Alden told Priscilla. "The ground is frozen—and so are our hands and feet!"

Soon the Common House became a kind of hospital. Most of the Pilgrims were sick. The few healthy men and women did the work for all. They worked willingly and cheerfully.

It was a very sad and difficult time. By the end of
February, only 12 or 14 Pilgrims were well. Priscilla's
family and many of the others died that first winter.
Alone now, Priscilla went to live with another family.

Spring brought new hope to the Pilgrims.

One fine day Priscilla was planting garden seeds. When she looked up, she couldn't believe her eyes. A tall Indian was walking up the path to the Common House. As he reached the door, he raised his hand in friendly greeting. ''Welcome!'' he said.

The Pilgrims were amazed.

''Welcome!'' answered William Bradford.

''What is your name? How did you learn to speak English?'' asked John Alden.

''My name is Samoset,'' he said.

Some English fishermen had taught Samoset to speak English. The Pilgrim men talked with him all afternoon. He did not leave until the next day.

A few weeks later, Samoset came to Plymouth again. This time he brought another Indian, named Squanto, with him. Squanto also spoke English.

"Welcome, Englishmen!" he said to the Pilgrims. "I will be your friend." And he was.

Squanto taught them many things that spring.
Early in April, the settlers began planting corn.
Squanto stopped them. "Your crop will not grow,"
he said. "First you must feed the soil."

Squanto showed them how to catch small fish in a
bucket. He put the fish in the ground with the corn.

"Now your corn crop will grow," he said. And it did.

He taught them about the best time to plant corn.

"Watch the oak leaves," he said. "Plant when the leaves are as big as a mouse's ear."

Squanto stayed in Plymouth and lived with the Pilgrims. They were very grateful for his help.

During this time the good Captain Jones made ready to sail back to England on the *Mayflower*.

"Will any of you come back with me?" he asked.

None of the Pilgrims chose to leave.

"So many of us have died. But we'll not give up," they said. "We know there are still hard times to come. But we will survive here."

The First Thanksgiving

Soon it was October. The corn had grown tall. The Pilgrims stored fruits and vegetables, meat and fish. They would have plenty of food in the coming winter.

There was no more terrible sickness.

One night Priscilla sat up in bed. "I can't sleep," she said to herself. "William Bradford says we'll have a day for giving thanks. There's so much to do!"

The next day, fires were lit. Women cooked.
They roasted wild turkeys and ducks and geese.
They bubbled soup and made stew and corn bread.
They baked strawberries and cherries in dough.
They popped corn just as Squanto had shown them.

The Pilgrims invited their Indian friends to share in their Thanksgiving Day. More than 90 of them came. They brought five deer to the feast.

Before the eating began, William Bradford said, "Let us give a prayer of thanks. Let us thank God for our food, for our Indian friends, and for this wonderful land."

Later there were many games.

The children cheered as John Alden and John Howland ran races with the Indian braves.

Miles Standish had the men march in a parade. In return the Indians did their dances for the Pilgrims.

They all promised friendship and good will.

The feasting lasted for three whole days!

The Pilgrim and the Indian leaders said they would have a Thanksgiving Day every year.

Priscilla smiled. "That's good," she thought. "But I will never forget this *first* Thanksgiving!"

The year after the first Thanksgiving, Priscilla and John Alden were married. They had 9 children.

Priscilla and John lived in Plymouth all their lives. Priscilla lived to be 83 years old. John lived to be 87.

They had many, many grandchildren, and great-grandchildren, and even great-great-grandchildren.

In fact, some of their descendants are living today.